Outdoor**IQ**

ULTIMATE

FiSHiNG guiDE

JUST FOR KIDS!

BY DAVE AND STEVE SHELLHAAS

MIAMI VALLEY OUTDOOR MEDIA, LTD.

OutdoorIQ

For more information
address the publisher:
Miami Valley Outdoor Media, Ltd.
P.O. Box 35
Greenville, Ohio 45331

978-0-9845251-1-9
Printed and bound in USA.

Photographs by Steve and Dave Shellhaas, and iStock photo stock

Disclaimer
All the Internet addresses (URLs) given in this book were valid at the time of going to press. However, due to the dynamic nature of the Internet, some addresses may have changed or ceased to exist since publication. While the authors and publisher regret any inconvenience this may cause readers, no responsibility for any such changes can be accepted by either the authors or the publisher.

CON

The Crappie

Common Crappie Names:

Specks, White Perch, Sac-a-lait, Croppie, Papermouth, Slabs

White Crappie or Black Crappie? What's the Difference?

WHITE CRAPPIE

There is less color on the side of the fish. It just has some specks or small lines of black.

The top fin has 5 or 6 spiny rays.

The measurement from the eye to the front of the top dorsal fin is MORE than the measurement from the back of the dorsal fin to the front of the dorsal fin.

BLACK CRAPPIE

The sides of the fish have dark black spots and markings. Sometimes it has more dark color than light.

The top fin has 7 or 8 spiny rays.

The measurement from the eye to the front of the top dorsal fin is the SAME as the measurement from the back of the dorsal fin to the front of the dorsal fin.

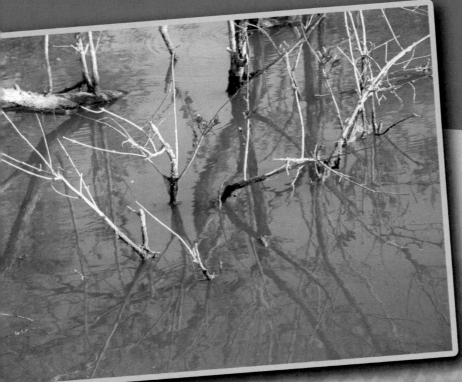

Habitat:

Crappie are usually found around standing timber and brushy cover in lakes. In the spring they inhabit the shallow ends of coves, later moving to water 15 or more feet deep.

Crappie Size:

World record black crappie is 5 pounds and the record white crappie is 5 pounds, 3 ounces. Most crappie caught are in the half to one pound range. Some states have a 9 or 10 inch size limit on crappie.

Natural Food Sources:

Minnows, shad, crayfish, mollusks, and insects.

Catchin' Crappie

Crappie Fishing Basics

Step 1

Pick your bobber
The best way to tell you have a bite is to use a bobber or float. This will show you when the fish takes the bait. As soon as the bobber goes under, the fish has taken your bait. Lift the rod and start reeling. IT MIGHT BE A BIG ONE!!

combination float

slip bobber

clip on bobber

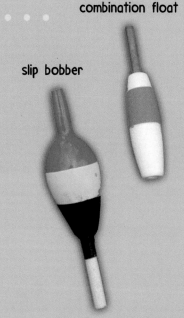

peg bobber

bare hook

plain jig

hair jig

curly tail jig

maribou jig

Step 2

Choose your hook or jig
You will never catch that crappie if there is nothing tied to your line. You can use many different jigs or hooks. Some are plain and some are colorful and made of funny things. BE CAREFUL!! These hooks are sharp!!

Step 3

Pick your bait
Crappies bite many kinds of bait. Minnows are good bait and so are waxworms. Be sure the bait is lively for the best action. The more action the bait has, the better action you may have catching fish!!

Step 4

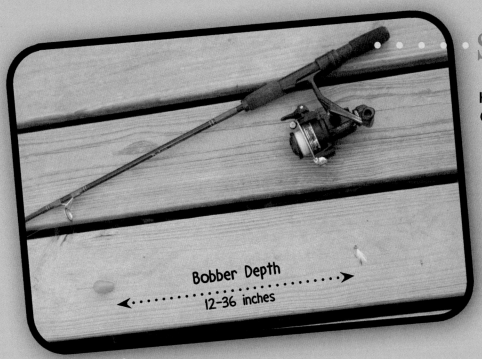

How Deep??
Crappies can be in shallow water in early spring. At those times you can set the bobber depth a few inches deep. As the water get warmer, the crappies move deeper. Then you can fish up to three feet deep or maybe even deeper. Once you find the depth the fish are biting, that is where you want to be!!

Bobber Depth
12-36 inches

Step 5

Where to Fish??
Crappies like to live by different structures. Fish by brush, stick ups, lily pads and boat docks. Sometimes crappies are found near rocks too.

Success!!

Step 6 • • • • • • • • • • • • • •

Catch that Fish!!
If you have done your homework and picked the right bobber, jig, bait and location, you should catch that crappie. Good Job!!

The Bluegill

©iStockphoto 2bgil

Common Bluegill Names

Bream, Brim or Sunfish

Identifying Bluegill:

Bluegills have one main feature that makes them easy to identify. That feature is the blue gill flap which is how the bluegill got its name.

blue gill flap

male bluegill

orange belly

What's the Difference between a male and a female bluegill?

The males have orange bellies while the females have a more yellowish belly.

female bluegill

yellow belly

Bluegill Size:

Most bluegills are between 6 to 10 inches long. They very rarely get bigger than 12 inches and usually weigh less than one pound.

The official world record bluegill is 4 pounds 12 ounces. However, a man caught a "hybrid" bluegill (a cross between a bluegill and a sunfish) by hand when he drained a pond. That fish weighed 5 pounds and would have been a world record if it was caught on a rod and reel.

Habitat:

Bluegill can be found from Texas to Minnesota to Florida and everywhere inbetween. Bluegills are quite common in warm-water shallow weedy ponds, lakes, and slow-moving streams. They seem to like the weedy shallows near shore.

Help! Don't eat me!

Natural Food Sources:

Insects, crustaceans, larvae and snails. Occasionally bluegill eat aquatic plants.

11

Bluegills on the Bed

"Secrets to Catching Bluegills Like Crazy"

Some of the best bluegill fishing of the year happens during May and June. As the weather warms up, so does the temperature of the water in many lakes and ponds. This tells the bluegills it is time to spawn.

What is spawning?

Spawning is when the female fish lays her eggs and the male fish fertilizes them. Many fish, like bluegills, make special places to lay their eggs. These are called spawning beds.

How do you find spawning beds?

The best place to find spawning beds is in shallow water. This is where the water is usually the warmest. You should also look for gravel or a sandy bottom.

Bluegills will make small areas that look like circles of rocks or gravel. You should be able to see the beds if the water is clear. If you look close, you will probably see the fish swimming in or around those beds.

Why do the fish stay by the spawning beds?

The reason the fish stay close to the spawning beds or nests is to protect the eggs and the developing baby fish. Many predators, such as salamanders, insects, crayfish and other fish, like to eat fish eggs and the baby fish.

The male fish guards the nest very seriously. The male will attack anything that comes near the spawning bed he is guarding.

The female fish will swim off into deeper water after they lay their eggs. So the fish you see on the spawn beds are usually the male fish unless the females are still there laying their eggs.

How does this help us catch them?

Because the male fish guards the nest or bed so aggressively, he will bite and attack anything that you put in or near the spawning bed. This makes them very easy to catch.

If you have the right set up on your fishing pole, HANG ON!! You will have nonstop action when those fish start attacking your bait.

What is the best pole to catch bluegills?

You can use many types of fishing poles to catch bluegills. The main thing is not to get too close to the spawning beds. If you get too close and the water is very clear, the fish will get scared of you and swim away.

The best thing to do is use a long cane pole or a fishing rod you can cast very well. You will need to stay far enough away not to scare the bluegill but be close enough you can cast to them or reach them with a long cane pole.

What set up works best to catch bluegills?

Spawning bluegills are usually in shallow water and you want to keep the bait in front of them so they can see it. This means you need to use a bobber or float to keep the hook and bait up off the bottom.

You may need to experiment with different depths to find the right distance between the float and bait. Once you find the right depth, you will know it.

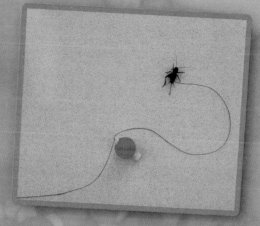

What baits work best?

At this time of year, the type of bait is not real important. Bluegills will attack about anything that comes near the bed. You can use small jigs such as ice jigs or 1/32 oz jigs. Poppers and artificial flies also work well.

You can also use bare hooks and live bait. Good live bait include waxworms, nightcrawlers, redworms, crickets and grasshoppers. Hook worms through the body a couple of times. Hook crickets and grasshoppers only one time through the body.

Get ready for some FAST action!

Once you find the right depth and have a bait that the fish like to attack, you will probably have a bite everytime your hook hits the water! You may get tired of pulling in the fish and taking them off the hook.

What is the best way to take a bluegill off the hook?

It may be best to have an adult help you take the fish off the hook to start with. However, with some practice and know-how, you can take the fish off the hook yourself.

Here are some tips:

1. Always wet you hands before you touch the fish, especially if you are going to return or release the fish back into the water. You can use a towel to help you but be sure it is wet. Dry hands and towels will wipe off the slime layer the fish has on its body. This slime layer is important protection for the fish. Without it, the fish may die if it is released back into the water.

2. Be sure the top, spiny dorsal fins are pushed back before you grab the fish. Those spines can hurt if they poke you!!

3. Hold the fish firmly while you take the hook out of the fish's mouth.

4. Use needle-nose pliers or hemistats(a tool a doctor uses) to grab the hook and take it out. These can really help if the fish swallows the hook deep into its mouth.

Important things to think about!!

Catching bluegills when they are on the spawning beds can be a lot of fun and the action can be fast. However, you need to remember that the reason you are catching so many is because they are protecting their eggs and babies.

Because bluegills reproduce very quickly, keeping a few bluegills to eat is okay. But, if you and several other people catch and keep too many, there will be no fish left to protect the eggs and baby fish. This can allow predators to come in and eat the eggs or young fish.

For this reason, it is sometimes good to practice "catch and release" at this time of year. This means you can catch as many fish as you want but return or release most of them back into the water so they can go back and protect their nest.

Get out there and have some fun catching "Bluegills on the Beds", just be sure you do your part so there will be more fish to catch in years to come!!

The Habitat Connection

Pond Habitat

Pond-a body of water smaller than a lake
A pond habitat is a common habitat found in many places. You can find ponds in parks. There are farm ponds found in the country. You can even make a small pond in your backyard. Ponds are home to many plants and animals.

Animals that live in a pond:
- fish like bass, bluegill and catfish
- painted and snapping turtles
- clams and mussels
- crayfish and tadpoles
- dragonfly and mosquito babies (larva)
- tiny, one-celled animals that you can't see with out a microscope

dragonfly

muskrat

painted turtle

frog in duckweed

Animals that live around a pond:
- birds like ducks, geese and blue herons
- frogs and toads
- muskrat and beaver
- raccoons and mink
- adult dragonflies and mosquitoes

Plants that live in and around a pond:
- cattails and reeds
- duckweed
- willow trees
- underwater plants like coontail, milfoil and eelgrass
- water lillies
- green slimy algae that people sometimes call "moss"

Ponds are really cool places to visit and explore. The next time you explore a pond, look for the plants and animals that live there. All of these living things depend on each other. Small animals and fish eat the different plants in and around the pond. Bigger animals eat the smaller animals. This makes up a food chain. There are many different food chains found in and around a pond. See if you can find some!

As you visit the pond, be sure not to damage the plants or disturb the animals that live there. Remember, it is home to many plants and animals. Many animals raise their families in and around ponds.

Whenever you visit any habitat, you should leave it the same way you found it!!

red-winged black bird with young

Largemouth Bass

(Micropterus salmoides)

▶ Largest member of the Sunfish family.

Also known as: Black bass, bigmouth, green bass, green trout, and bucketmouth.

▶ Color ranges from light to dark green to sometimes black bodies with grey-white bellies. Dark line in middle of body that goes from gills to tail is known as the lateral line.

▶ Upper jaw goes past the back edge of the eye.

▶ Females grow larger than males.

Rounded tail and notched fin

Deep notch in fin

Lateral line

Golden-brown eye

You can now catch

Largemouth bass from the east coast to the west coast, and from Canada to Mexico.

World Record Largemouth Bass - 22 lbs 4 oz. caught in Georgia (1932).

Largemouth bass live about 10 to 15 years in the wild.

16

Largemouths bass like warm, slow moving, shallow, and weedy water. They are usually found in water less than 20 feet in depth.

Bass also like to be by structure. This means they like to live by objects under the water, such as logs, stumps, rocks, brush piles, and docks.

Hiding in structure allows the bass to jump out and catch its food.

Largemouths bass will eat about anything that can fit in its mouth. They like to eat smaller fish, crawdads, snakes, salamanders, mammals, and even birds.

The Largemouth bass is the most popular fish to catch in North America.

▶ **Bass use one of 5 senses:**

Vision: Bass can see in every direction except below and behind them. They can see in color when in clear water.

Smell/Taste: Bass can smell and taste, but use these senses the least.

Hearing/Touch: Bass can hear noises underwater with their internal ears. They also have a lateral line that helps them feel vibrations in the water. This helps them feel the movements of fish or food in the water.

Big Bobbers for Big Bass!

▶ **First, get your bait. You can buy your bait, or catch it yourself.**

Go to your local stream and seine shiners and chubs.
Keep the fish that are 4-6 inches in length.

Big hooks: can use several types of hooks, but need to be big enough to keep the bait on the hook.

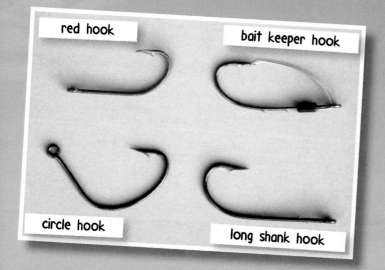

red hook

bait keeper hook

circle hook

long shank hook

Big Bobbers: the bobber has to be big enough to keep your bait from pulling the bobber under.

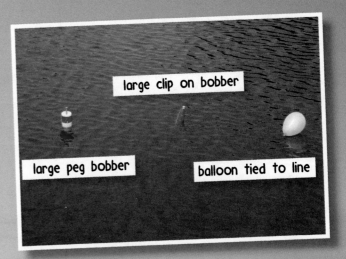

large clip on bobber

large peg bobber

balloon tied to line

Simple Set-up: bobber, weight, and hook.

Set bobber 18-36 inches, make sure bait is not sitting on the bottom.

Hook bait through the nose or behind the dorsal fin.

▶ Catch Some Bass!

Cast out by stumps, brush, weeds, or rocks. Watch the bobber closely.

The bobber will move all around because of the big shiner or chub minnow swimming around. When the bobber goes completely under, reel up the loose line and set the hook.

Tips and Tricks

▶ Make sure your bait stays lively, the more they move the more bass you will catch

▶ Let the bass take the bobber under for 2-3 seconds before you set the hook.

▶ Farm ponds are great places to catch bass.

▶ Catch your bass, take a picture, and then release the bass to fight another day.

Awesome Bass!!

Stars in the ★ Outdoors

KVD - Kevin Vandam

★★★★★

If you follow the sport bass fishing, you should know that Kevin Vandam, or KVD as he is sometimes known, is one of the best bass fishermen in the history of the sport. He won the B.A.S.S. Angler of the Year award during his first year on the pro circuit (1992), and again in 1996, 1999 and 2008. That makes FOUR Angler of the Year awards!! That is awesome!!

In 2001, he won the FLW Angler of the Year title, and in 2004 and 2005 Kevin became the first Elite 50 champion. He also won the Bassmaster Classic championship which is the Superbowl of bass fishing in 2001 and 2005. Wow!! Now that is one good bass fisherman!!

OutdoorIQ (OIQ) interview with KVD:

OIQ: What age did you start fishing and hunting? Who got you started fishing and hunting?

KVD: I started hunting with my Dad and my brother when I was 5 years old. I really was their "dog" when I went along rabbit and pheasant hunting. As far as fishing, I started fishing at age 3 by ice fishing with my Dad.

OIQ: Did you always want to be a professional fisherman? How did you get into pro fishing?

KVD: No, I really did not set out to be a professional fisherman and never had that as a goal. I have always loved fishing and I am very competitive and like to compete. That led me to enter my first fishing tournament at age 14. I then joined a bass club at age 16 and began fishing more tournaments. Eventually that led me to where I am today.

OIQ: What other things do you like to do in the outdoors?

KVD: I love all types of hunting. I enjoy hunting ducks, geese, rabbits and squirrel. I also like to take at least one trip a year and go hunting. I am looking forward to elk hunting this fall. But my passion is whitetail hunting and turkey hunting. I have always loved to deer hunt!

OIQ: What is your favorite lure to catch fish and why?

KVD: It has to be the spinnerbait. It is my favorite lure because it is so versatile. You can fish it shallow or deep, in open water or in heavy cover. Basically you can fish it anywhere and it catches fish.

OIQ: What is your favorite game to hunt and why?

KVD: As I mentioned earlier, my passion is hunting the whitetail deer. It is my favorite animal to hunt because it is so challenging to hunt. There is nothing tougher to hunt than an old whitetail buck. I also like deer because they are so unique and different. No two bucks ever look the same. Their antlers each have their own shape and look.

OIQ: Is there a favorite or funny fishing or hunting memory you would like to share?

KVD: A memory that stands out is a hunting memory when I was younger. We always hunted northern Michigan. The bucks don't grow real big in northern Michigan but we still loved to hunt them. Michigan had a 2 buck limit and on a trip when I was 14 years old with my Dad I had a great hunt. We went out bowhunting one morning and I filled both of my buck tags in 15 minutes. I shot a 4 pointer and a 6 pointer and was very excited. When my Dad came up to get me he wasn't sure what was wrong because the way I was acting and then I told him my story of getting both bucks in 15 minutes of the hunt. That is a great memory!

OIQ: What would you tell a young person who would like to be professional fisherman to do?

KVD: Well, obviously they need to learn how to fish but that is not the most important thing. Education is probably the most important thing. It is important to do well in school, graduate and go onto college. Most guys on the circuit today have college degrees in some field. So fish a lot yes, but also be sure to get a good education.

Seine

Materials Needed:

- 2 yards of netting material
- 2 - three foot long, 1/2 inch diameter wooden dowel rods
- 6 - round, clip-on bobbers
- several 1/2 ounce split-shot weights
- pliers • measuring tape • scissors • stapler

Step 1

Lay out the netting material on a flat surface.

Measure and cut the netting so it is two feet wide and four feet long.

Step 2

Wrap the ends of the netting around each dowel rod 2-3 times. Be sure to keep the bottom of the netting even with the bottom of the dowel rod.

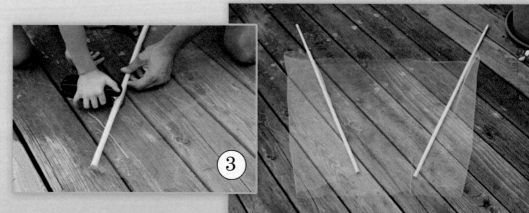

Step 3

Next, staple the netting to the dowel rod using a stapler. Put a staple about every 1-2 inches on each side of the dowel rod.

Step 4

Using pliers, crimp several split-shot weights across the bottom of the seine. Be sure to space the weights evenly across the bottom.
An adult may need to help you do this.

These will help keep the seine on the bottom of the stream when you use it.

This is FUN!

Step 5

Next, have someone fold over the top edge of the netting and hold it for you. Then, take six round, clip-on bobbers and clip them across the top of the netting. Again, try to space the bobbers equally across the top of the seine.

The bobbers will keep the top of the seine floating on the surface of the water when it is used in the stream.

GREAT!!
You now should have a finished seine. You can roll up the seine and carry it to the stream.

You can use the seine to catch minnows, crayfish and other creatures that live in the stream.

Using Your Seine:

You can have one person on each end of the seine while you try to catch bait or you can roll the seine up a little and hold it yourself. Face upstream and have your friends walk toward you as they shuffle their feet on the bottom of the stream. When they get in front of the seine quickly lift it out of the water and see what you caught!!!

*SAFETY NOTE:
Always be sure an adult is there to help you when you use your seine. NEVER go into a deep, fast moving stream. Stay in shallow areas where there is slow, flowing water.

Channel Catfish

Color: Silvery blue to light olive, with black spots
Spots disappear as the channel gets old

Fins: Deeply forked tail, and less than 30 rays in the anal fin. This fin is also more rounded. The fin on the top (dorsal fin) and the fins on the side (pectoral fins) have very sharp, pointy spines and can hurt you. Be Careful!!

Skin: Channel catfish have skin, no scales
The catfish have long, pointy whiskers that are really called barbels. Although they look like they could hurt you, they are safe to touch. They use these whiskers to smell and find food at night.

Average size: weighs 2 to 7 pounds and 12 to 24 inches in length.

Feeding Habits:

Channel catfish mainly feed on the bottom and mostly at night.

They use taste buds in their nose, skin and whiskers. This allows them to feed at night in total darkness.

Catfish are scavengers which means that they will eat anything dead or alive. They eat worms (nightcrawlers), minnows, frogs, and other fish.

Deeply Forked Tail

Spots appear on sides of young fish

Less Than 30 Rays In Anal Fin

Rounded Outer Marg

Where do Channel Cats Live?

They can live in lakes, rivers, streams, and ponds. They like to live in places with sandy, rocky, or gravel bottoms.

Catfish are located in the Central, Eastern United States, and Southern Canada

How to Catch One?

• **Rod and reel:** using a variety of baits from chicken livers, nightcrawlers, soap, hot dogs, dough balls, and store bought baits.

• **By hand!!!** Some people reach into logs and holes underwater and catch catfish using their hands. This is called noodling or grabbling. Don't try this at Home!!

• **Trotline:** This is a long line with several hooks on the line that are left in the water and checked daily. There are rules for trotlines in each state, check the law first.

• **Jug fishing:** A large jug or bottle has fishing line, a hook, and bait attached to the jug. The jug is left out overnight and checked daily.

Did You Know . . .
The world record Channel Catfish was caught in South Carolina weighing a whopping 58 pounds!

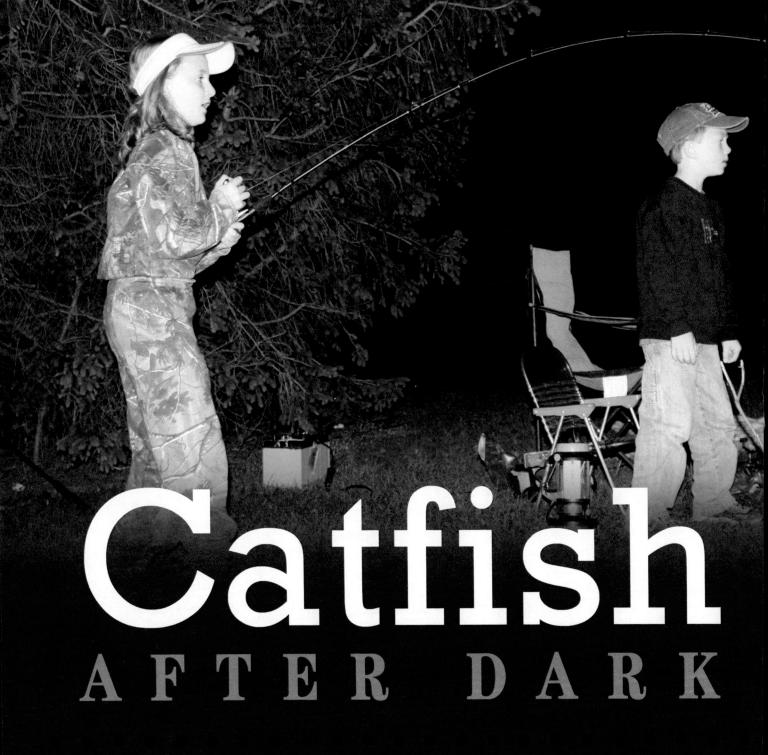

Catfish
AFTER DARK

Why fish at night?

Channel catfish are more active at night, especially during the summer.

At night, catfish come into shallow water and are easier to catch.

What do I need to Night Fish?

- Strong Rod and reel- these fish are strong
- Lights/headlamp- to see in the dark
- Bug repellent- to keep the bugs off
- Chair or blanket- to help relax and enjoy
- Prop stick- to hold your pole up
- Bait- lots of choices to catch the big one
- Net- to land the fish

Best Ways to Fish?

Tight-Line- this is when your bait sits on the bottom. You do not use a bobber and you must watch your line to know if you have a bite.

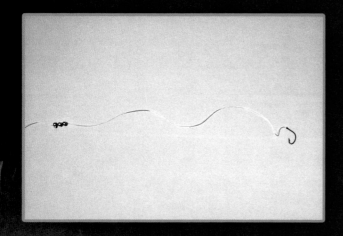

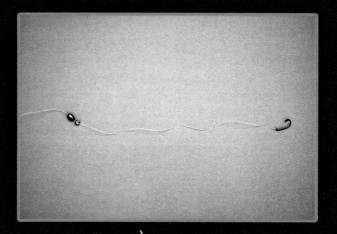

Split shot rig
Easy to use, just squeeze 2-3 Split shots onto the line about 18 inches from the hook.

Carolina rig
Allows fish to take the bait without feeling any weight. Slide on 1/4 oz. barrel sinker, then a split shot about 18-20 inches from the hook.

Bobber fishing- this is using a bobber to keep bait off the bottom, and allows you to see when you have a bite.

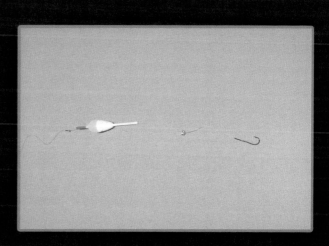

Lighted Bobber
Makes the bobber glow and

Slip bobber rig
Harder to set up, but you

Types of Baits to use:

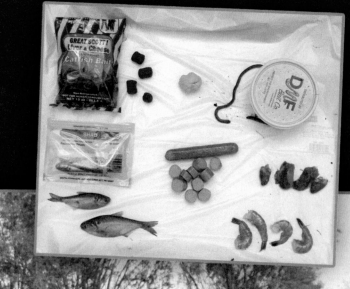

- Worms, chicken livers, dough balls, cut bait
- Shrimp, home made baits, hot dogs
- Store bought baits, soap, and cheese

Poles at an angle, so you can watch your line and rod tip

Light/lantern

Chairs

Prop stick

It is a good idea to set up when it is still light out.

At night, you must watch your rod, line, or bobber. A strong catfish can pull your rod and reel into the lake in just a few seconds.

So, when the line gets tight, your rod tip bends, or your bobber goes down: Set the hook and hold on!!!

The Habitat Connection

Rivers

River- a large flowing body of freshwater water flowing toward a lake or ocean.

How do rivers form?
Rivers form when small streams and creeks join together. The smaller rivers and streams that join to make a large river are called **tributaries**.

Why are rivers important to animals?
Rivers are important for many different animals because they provide water and food. Many animals like deer drink water from rivers. Other animals like bear and raccoons find their food in the river.

Birds like kingfishers and herons hunt for fish in the river. The bank of the river provides home for animals like beaver, muskrat and mink.

What animals live in the river?
Many different types of fish live in rivers. Catfish, bass and panfish live in many rivers. Crayfish and mussels can aso be found in the river. Many baby insects (larva) spend the first part of their life under rocks and on plants found in the river.

Rivers are also a wonderful place for people to visit and explore. You can enjoy fishing, boating or canoeing in rivers. It is important that we all do our part in keeping rivers clean and beautiful. Be sure to never leave any trash behind when you visit a river. You can also help keep rivers clean by picking up any garbage you may see by a river that was left by someone else.

Remember, it is up to us to take care of our rivers. Rivers are not only a great place for us to enjoy, they are also provide food and a home for many different animals. Let's all work hard to keep all of our rivers beautiful.

Catfishing Gear and Tips

Making a propstick: a propstick helps keep your pole upright to help see if you have a bite

The prop stick being used at the pond.

① Pick a tree branch that has a Y and about 18-24 inches of straight wood. Have your parent cut the branch from the tree.

② Trim the branch at the marks above.

Making a Lantern Kid Friendly:
this tip keeps the light out of your eyes, and allows you to see better.

① Take a sheet of aluminum foil and wrap it half-way around the lantern glass. Make sure to do this when the lantern is off.

② This makes all the light go out the front and keeps the light out of your eyes. This also keeps the bugs away from you too.

Other Gear that makes Night Fishing Easier:

Headlamps: • • • • • • • • • • • •
always have a light ready to take fish
off, change bait, or watch your line.

• • • • • • • • **Lighted bobbers:**
this bobber has a light inside so you can see it
at night. When the bobber/light disappears, you
have a bite.

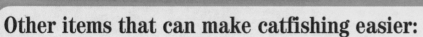

Other items that can make catfishing easier:
• Wet wipes to keep your hands clean • Pliers to help remove hooks
• A scale to weigh your trophy catfish • Extra hooks and weights ready to use
• A camera to take your picture

Catfish Bait Recipes

Although there are a lot of good catfish baits you can buy in the stores, sometimes it is fun to make your own. Here are some fun recipes that you can try to make. We are sure Mom will love helping you make these wonderful recipes so you can go out and catch big catfish!!

Catfish Cornflakes

Ingredients:
Corn Flakes, water, cheese powder from Mac and Cheese mix, creamy peanut butter

Directions:
1. Crush up the corn flakes.
2. Add enough water to the crushed corn flakes until it looks like play-dough. (You should be able to make it into a ball.)
3. Let it sit for 5 minutes. Add the powdered cheese and mix well.
4. Then add peanut butter and mix very well.
5. Freeze the mixture until you are ready to fish.

Hotdog Bait

Ingredients:
six pack of really cheap hotdogs, garlic salt, anise extract, vanilla extract
Other ingredients to try:
teriyaki or vinegar, brown sugar, seasoned salt, parmesan cheese

Directions:
1. Cut hotdogs up into lots of small pieces.
2. Put all the chopped pieces in a jar or zipper bag and pour some vanilla, anise extract and garlic salt.
3. Mix up and let the hot dogs soak for an hour or so.
Experiment by adding teriyaki or vinegar, powdered iced tea, brown sugar, seasoned salt or parmesan cheese.

32

Catfish Corn Bait

Ingredients:
Can of whole corn
Vanilla extract

Directions:
1. Drain the water from the can of corn and leave only about 5 percent water in the can.
2. Pour enough vanilla in the can until the corn turns a brownish-yellow color (use your own judgement).
3. Shake the can, and let the vanilla absorb into the corn.
4. Depending on your hook,(a #2 treble hook is good), you should be able to slide on about 4 or 5 good sized pieces of corn.

A Cleaner Bait

1. Take a bar of soap and have a grown up put the soap on a paper plate and put it in the microwave for 25-30 seconds.
2. This will make the soap soft enough to cut. Cut the soap into pieces about the size of ping pong ball.
3. Stick a toothpick in the pieces and dip them in a little bit of vanilla extract or red soda pop.
4. Put them in the freezer overnight and then put them in the fridge until you go fishing.

Thanks to Bobberstop.com for these fun recipes. Check out bobberstop.com for fishing information of all kinds. You can find more bait recipes and other fishing tips at this great site.

Yellow Perch

(Perca Flavescens)

Also known as ringed perch, lake perch, and raccoon perch

▶ Yellowish-green sides with 6-9 vertical dark bars
White or cream colored bellies, with orange colored lower fins.

▶ Females are not as bright colored as males.

▶ Perch are the smaller cousins of the Walleye and Sauger.

▶ Travel in Schools, usually are similar in size
(If you catch a small perch, most in that school will be small)

Averages:

Length- 5-12 inches
Weight- 0.25 to 1 pound

World Record Yellow Perch

4 pounds 3 ounces.
Caught in New Jersey, 1865.

Diet:

• Perch eat insects, crawfish, snails, small fish, and fish eggs.

• Perch eat mainly during daylight hours, early morning and late evening.

Use small minnows, worms, leeches, crickets, or grubs to help catch perch.

Where do perch live?

• Perch live from South Carolina to Kansas, and north into Canada.

• They prefer clear water with a lot of weeds, sand and gravel bottoms.

• Usually perch are in water less than 30 foot deep.

Perch use their spiny dorsal fins to help protect them from other fish.

Be careful, they can hurt you too.

35

Perch
Fishing Great Family Fun!

 **Perch** are not only fun to catch, they are great eating. You can find perch in many deep lakes and even in a few ponds. Try your luck at catching these tasty fish and you will have a blast.

What do you use?

The most common way to catch perch is to use a rig called a "perch spreader". This is a set up that has two hooks and many times a flashy blade to get the perch's attention. You can use minnows or shiners on the hooks as bait.

How do you catch them?

On large lakes, it is best to use a boat with a fish finder to find schools of perch. Once a school of yellow perch is found, it is best to anchor and fish near the bottom using shiners or minnows. A large weight is used to get the hook and shiner to the bottom and then the bait is worked up and down off the bottom until a perch takes the bait. Raising the rod tip will set the hook and then just reel the perch in.

In ponds, the perch also like cooler water. Early mornings or evenings are typically the best time to catch pond perch. They will stay around structure like trees or rock pile. One of the best ways to catch pond perch is to use a slip bobber and a small hook with a minnow or shiner. By moving the slip bobber stopper, you can change the depths at which you fish to find the depth the yellow perch are using to feed.

There is not much to catching perch once you find them. Perch swim in schools which means they travel together. Once you find a school and catch one perch. There are many more down there to be catch.

Keep your perch rigs baited and hang on!! With any luck at all, you will bring home a nice mess of perch to fry and share with your family.

Saugeye

A saugeye is half walleye and half sauger.

- Member of the Perch family
- World Record is 15.66 pounds, caught in Montana.

Average length:
13-16 inches
Average weight:
1-2 pounds

©istock/Roman Ponomarev

Habitat: able to live in many different types of lakes and rivers, and can even live in muddy waters.

Food: from the time they are young, saugeyes mainly eat other smaller fish.

Most saugeyes are raised in a fish hatchery, and then stocked into lakes and rivers when they are only a few inches long.

Since the Saugeye is part walleye and part sauger, they look like both fish.

Sometimes it is hard to tell the difference between a sauger, walleye, and saugeye. Here are a few ways to help.

A SAUGEYE WILL HAVE:

A spotted dorsal fin (the fin on top of the fish)

Dark blotches on the side of the fish

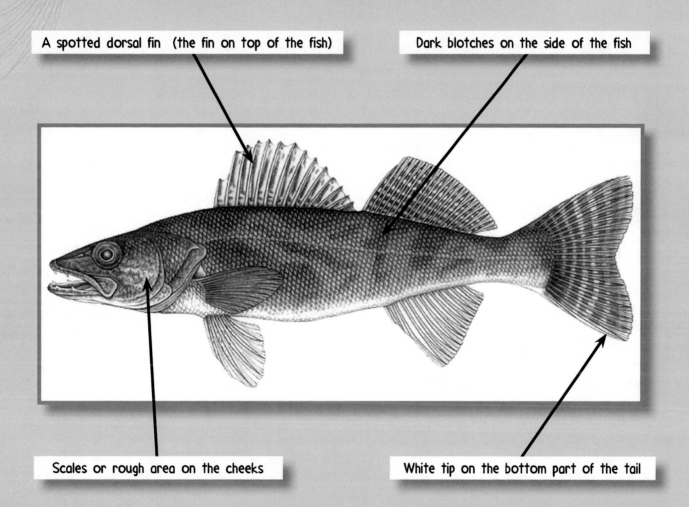

Scales or rough area on the cheeks

White tip on the bottom part of the tail

Saugeyes can be caught in rivers, tailwaters, lakes, and even through the ice during the winter.

Be careful when touching a saugeye, do not put your fingers in their mouths because they have very sharp teeth!

Wintertime Saugeyes

FISHING SPILLWAYS

What is a Spillway?

A Spillway is a passageway where extra water escapes from a lake or Reservoir.

In the Winter, the best place to fish for saugeye is in the tailwaters.

Where are the Tailwaters?

Tailwater is the water immediately downstream from a spillway.

The tailwater is made from water being released or flowing through the spillway. This happens more after a big rain.

GEAR

- Rod and Reel
- Lead head jigs
- Twister tails in several colors.
- Net and warm clothes
- Life jacket

How to fish

- Cast your jig upstream.
- Then start reeling in after counting from 1 to 10 seconds depending on how deep the tailwater is.
- When you count, the jig sinks about 1 foot for every second you count.
- Count to different depths until you get a bite, make sure you remember what you counted to.

BE CAREFUL!

When fishing spillways in the winter, always wear your life jacket.

The water will be very cold and you will be wearing a lot of clothes, this makes swimming impossible.

Watch your step, take your time, and wear your life jacket.

Bites can be very light, so pay close attention to your rod tip and line.

Do not be afraid to set the hook when you think you have a bite.

Good luck, and stay warm

STAYING SAFE IN COLD WEATHER

Wintertime can be a lot of fun in many places in the United States. Whether you are playing in the snow or icefishing with a grown up, you need to keep some cold weather, safety tips in mind before you go outside or fishing on that frozen lake or pond.

Tips for staying safe in the cold:

- Be careful going outside when it is very windy. Although a thermometer may read 40 degrees, if the wind is blowing 20 miles per hour it can cause your body to lose heat as if the temperature were actually 18 degrees.

- Always try to cover any part of your skin that is showing when it is very cold. Leaving your skin uncovered in very cold weather can lead to frost bite.

- Dress in layers, and add extra clothing for the head, neck, and sides where your body loses the most heat. Wool and man-made fabrics are good choices for clothing. Cotton clothing is very slow to dry when it gets wet and can cause you to become very cold.

Tips for staying safe on the ice:

- Always go icefishing or onto a frozen lake or pond with a grown up!

- Always remember that ice-covered water is never completely safe.

- **Wear a Coast Guard-approved life jacket or float coat whenever you go out on the ice. Life vests provide excellent flotation and protection from hypothermia.**

43

Brown Trout
(Salmo trutta)

Brown Trout Facts

- First lived in Europe and Asia.

- Brown trout were brought to the United States over 100 years ago.

- Smartest of the trout family.

- Can live in warmer water than most other trout and salmon.

- Average size: 13 – 16 inches.

Where do they live?

- Brown trout like to live in streams and lakes.

- They like water that is cool and well oxygenated (has a lot of oxygen), and temperatures 40°F to 70°F.

What do they eat?

- Trout will eat water insects, smaller fish, crayfish, even many land insects and animals.

How can you tell it is a Brown Trout?

▶ The trout has a square type tail.

▶ Tails of brown trout have few spots

▶ Sometimes have red spots along the middle of fish.

▶ Black spots on their sides, back, and dorsal fins, each spot has a light halo around the spot.

▶ Olive green to brown on top of the fish

▶ Creamy to golden yellow on the fish sides, and an off white color on the belly.

Let's go trout fishing!!

What you need:

- Light spinning or spincast rod and reel
- Fishing line 4 to 6 pound test
- Small hooks, #10 to #14
- Few small split shot weights

Bait:

- Nightcrawlers are a very good bait.
- They are easy to cast and easy to find.
- You can also use spinners, jigs, and minnow imitating baits.

Worm Hint:

Cut the worm in half, and hook it once through the end of the worm. Try to hide the hook in the worm.

How to fish a stream:

1 Find a **pool**- this is a deep area of slower moving water after rapids.

2 Walk up to the pool from **downstream** –
this is walking the opposite direction of the current of the stream.

3 Move slowly, stay on land, and try to hide from the fish.

• Trout scare very easily and will not bite if they see you.

4 Cast upstream past the pool, and allow your bait to drift back to you.

• Your bait will bounce on the bottom as it comes back.

47

Tips to Remember!!

1 Reel slowly as your bait drifts back to you.

  • Try to reel all the loose line in when the bait is coming back toward you. This is called keeping the slack out of your line. When your line does not have any slack in it, it makes it easier to set the hook when you get a bite. This means you CATCH more FISH!!

2 Watch your line, when it moves or jerks this means you have a bite.

3 Make good casts. A bad cast can scare the fish and they will not bite.

4 Try to hide the hook when putting the worm on, this makes it look more realistic.

Good luck and have fun!

The Habitat Connection

Stream - a small body of flowing water
    - also called a brook or creek
A stream habitat is a common habitat that can be found
almost everywhere. Streams are usually narrow and fast
flowing with rocky and gravel bottoms. These peaceful,
flowing habitats are home to many animals.

crayfish

Animals that live in streams:
• fish like trout, salmon, sunfish, smallmouth and rock
  bass, and many types of minnows and shiners.
• softshell and snapping turtles • clams and mussels
• crayfish • dragonfly and other insect babies (larva)

Animals that live near streams:
• birds like wood ducks, kingfishers and blue herons
• river otters, muskrat and beaver • raccoons and mink
• adult dragonflies and mosquitoes

riffle

Parts of a Stream
Riffle - a shallow, rocky area with
fast flowing water.

Pool - a deeper area of a stream
where the flow is very slow.

Run - this area is shallower than
a pool and flows a little faster

woodduck

river otter

Streams are very beautiful but are in trouble in many places. Stream habitats
can be damaged when many of the trees and plants next to the stream are
removed. This allows soil and other things to wash into the stream and causes
the water to become muddy and is not good for the animals living in the stream.

Trees next to the stream also keep the water cool and shades the stream.
In places where the trees have been cut down, many fish, like trout, have
disappeared because the water is too warm.

It is very important that we do our part in protecting these wonderful habitats.
Get out there and explore the stream near you!!!

The Blue Crab

Okay, the blue crab is not a fish but it does spend its whole life in the water. The blue crab is actually a crustacean. Crustaceans belong to a group of animals called arthropods. Other crustaceans include lobsters, shrimp, and crayfish.

The main thing that all arthropods have in common is that they do not have bones or a skeleton. They have an exoskeleton with means its skeleton is on the outside of the body.

How do you tell a boy crab from a girl crab?

A boy or male crab has a shape on the bottom of its abdomen that is shaped like the Washington Monument.

They also have blue claws.

A young or immature girl or female crab has a shape on the bottom of its abdomen that is an upside down V.

They have orange or red claws.

An older or mature girl or female crab has a shape on the bottom of its abdomen that is shaped like the Capitol Building.

They have orange or red claws.

Parts of the Crab

carapace/shell

swimming legs

eyes

mouth

legs

claws

How do crabs grow?
Crabs grow by molting. Molting is when the crab sheds its exoskeleton. Because their hard skeleton is on the outside, the only way it can grow bigger is to get rid of the old shell or exoskeleton and grow a bigger one.

What do crabs eat?
Crabs eat thin shelled clams and oysters, worms, small fish, plants and about anything else they can find, including dead fish and other blue crabs.

Cool Crab Fact:
Soft shell crabs are crabs that are caught before their exoskeleton or shell has time to harden after it molts. People like to catch these crabs to eat!!

A Big Blue Crab!!
One blue crab was 11 inches across its shell and was from the Virginia Institute of marine studies.

Coastal Fun
FOR THE Whole Family

Whether you live near the coast or just visit there on vacation, there is a fun, family-friendly activity you can all do together. There are unique charters that take kids out along the coastal waters to catch shrimp, crabs and other interesting creatures.

Have you ever wondered where the seafood you eat come from?

Commercial fisherman use nets that drag along the bottom and catch the shrimp, crabs, fish and other sea creatures. Some commercial fishermen like Captain Russell from Gandpa's Shrimp and Crab Charters make their living fishing for shrimp and crabs.

OutdoorIQ went out with Capt. Russell to catch some shrimp and crabs near the Outer Banks of North Carolina.

Once out on the water, the first thing we did was drop the nets into the water and pulled the nets along the bottom.

Capt. Russell gets the nets ready.

Watching the net as it is pulled behind the boat.

Capt. Russell pulls the net in.

52

What did we catch??

After the net is pulled in, Capt. Russell empties the net on the sorting table.

Shrimp Anyone??

One thing we caught were **shrimp**. Shrimp are a prized seafood. You can find shrimp on any seafood menu and they are not cheap.

horn

Live shrimp have a sharp, pointy horn on the top of their head. You have to be careful when you handle live shrimp. That horn can poke and hurt you if you are not careful.

As you can see, shrimp come in many sizes. The large ones are the shrimp that are more expensive in the stores.

What out for the pinchers!!

We also caught **blue crabs** in the nets. Fresh crabs are also a prized seafood treat along the coast.

Capt. Russell showed us how to hold the crabs so they could not pinch us. He was so sure, he even held one in his mouth!!

Nap time for the crab!

Capt. Russell also showed us how to put a crab to sleep. He turned the crab upside down and rubbed its belly.

He then put the crab upside down and laid it on the edge of the table. It just laid there!! Was it really asleep???

How big do crabs have to be to keep them?

In North Carolina, you can only keep mature females and males with a shell (carapace) of more than 5 inches.

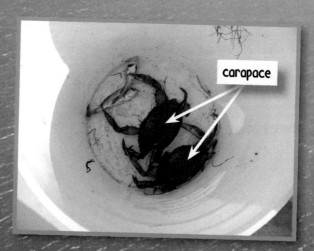

carapace

Capt. Russell's daughter Blare with two crabs.

54

Other Cool Things Caught

Shrimp and crabs were not the only neat things the net caught. We also caught some really unusual looking fish and sea creatures.

a squid

Is that you Squidward Tentacles?

No, it is just a **squid** with some squirmy tentacles that was caught by the net.

Squid Fact:

Squid have spots called chromatophores that change with the squids mood. Squid use these chromatophores to talk to each other and let other squid know how they feel.

squid with spots (chromatophores)

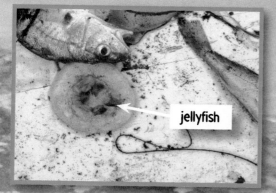

jellyfish

What is that blob?

It is a **jellyfish**. Jellyfish are also sometimes caught in the nets. You have to be careful with jellyfish. Some types have stings that are painful or can cause you to get very sick.

Besides catching shrimp and crabs with a net, you can also catch fish the normal way. Many of these charters will also take you and your family fishing.

You may not want to kiss the fish though!!

55

GETTIN' CRABBY

Catching blue crabs can be fun.
With some simple equipment and a little know how, you to can catch blue crabs the next time you are near the coast.

One way to catch blue crabs is to use a crab trap or crab pot. These are usually made of some type of wire.

You put bait in the trap. The bait can be a fish or raw chicken. The bait needs to be connected to the trap so the crabs cannot carry the bait away.

Once you bait the crab trap, you put it into the water where you know crabs are found. Good places to put your crab traps include public bridges, walkways, piers, docks or other shallow water areas where you have permission.

You lower the trap into the water and wait. After some time, the crabs will smell the bait and crawl into the trap.

Lowering the trap into the water.

Crab trap in the water. Make sure the doors are all down so the crabs can crawl in.

Watch the trap if you can and wait for the crab to get into the trap. When it does, pull it up quickly.

If you are quick enough, you will trap the crab and you can pull it up and see your catch. The crab will be caught inside the trap and then you will need to get it out.

Another way of catching crabs is to but some bait on a bait clip and then put the bait into the water. The crab will grab the bait with its claws and hold onto the bait.

Quickly and carefully, pull the bait and the crab up. Using a crab net (a net with a long handle), put the net under the crab as you pull it up and try to catch the crab in the net before it lets go.

This takes a lot of practice and patience. Many times the crab lets go before you can get the net under it.

bait clip

Blue crab with the bait on the bait clip.

Don't get too "crabby" if you have trouble catching the sneaky blue crab the first couple of times.

With some practice, you will soon be catching those pesky crabs and they do make a great meal if you know how to cook them!!

Good luck!

57

Crabbing Equipment

crab net

bait clip

crab trap

The crab pot or crab trap is the easiest way to catch crabs. The trap is baited and the crabs crawl in to eat the bait and get trapped inside.

The bait clip holds a bait like a fish or piece of raw chicken. The crab net has a long handle so you can reach down and try to catch the crab as it holds onto the bait when you pull it up.

ULTIMATE Fishing TECHNIQUES, TACKLE AND TIPS

When the temperature gets hot, go cool off in the streams.

Hot Stream Fishing

Put on some old shoes, shorts, shirt, sunscreen, and hat. Grab your rod and reel and some bait. Then start wading in the creek to catch some fish.

Use very small hooks or jigs with a small bobber.

Use live bait, either wax worms or small night crawlers.

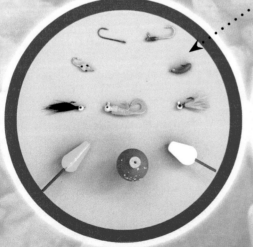

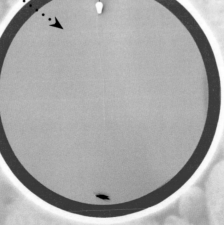

Read the Stream

Look for fast moving rapids. ·······································

There is usually deeper, slower moving water after the rapids. This is the first place to start fishing. ··············

Also look for any cover, such as stumps, rocks, or weeds.

Water current ◄ ·············

When stream fishing, there are two ways to cast.

① Standing on the bank, cast upstream, and let the water current bring your bait to the fish.
② When wading, also cast upstream. This keeps the water clean and prevents scaring any fish.

SAFETY:
① Always fish with an adult
② If the water is deep or fast-moving then wear a life jacket.
③ Watch your step, rocks will be slippery!!

What Can You Catch?

Can catch about anything; chubs, shiners, rockbass, catfish, sunfish, and bass.

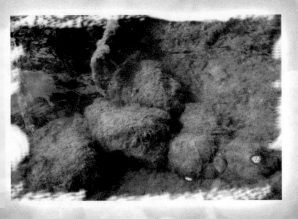

If the fish are not biting, there are a lot of ways to have fun in a stream.

61

Reels

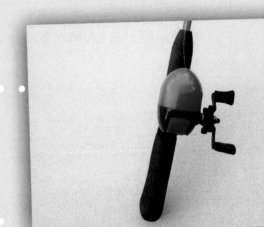

Spincast Reel:

- easy to cast
- great for beginners
- just push the button, and then let go to cast

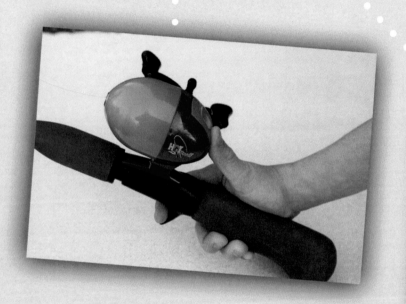

Underspin Reel:

- easy to use
- good for beginners and older kids.
- just pull trigger, then let go to cast

Spinning Reel:

- harder to use
- comes in different sizes
- must hold the line with finger to cast

Baitcaster reel:

- hardest to use
- use to cast, flip, and pitch
- use thumb to cast and control the line

CANE POLES

Definition: a fishing pole made of bamboo, fiberglass, or other material where line is tied to the end of the pole. No reel is used and casting is done by swinging or dropping the bait at a target.

Come in lengths from 10 to 20 feet.

WOW, THAT IS LONG!!

Made of bamboo or fiberglass, and can be 1-4 pieces or telescopic (means the sections all slide into each other and can be pull out until it is very long).

Easy and fun to use.

Easy to set up, cast, and catch fish.

Can catch bluegills, crappies, bass, and catfish.

How to Set Up Your Cane Pole:

If you are using a bamboo pole, tie the line 2 feet from tip and wrap line up to the tip of the pole.

Use 10-14 pound test monofilament fishing line.

The fishing line should be as long as the cane pole.

Use a small hook, sinker, and float. Live bait such as worms, crickets, and minnows work the best.

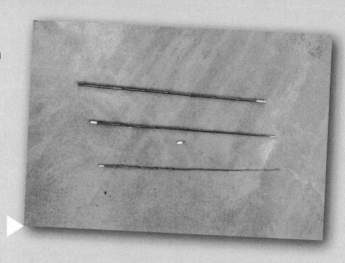

12 o'clock

2 o'clock

How to Cast:

• Use a swinging action to cast.
• As you face the water, pretend the cane pole is a hand on a clock.

• Let's say if you point the pole straight out in front of you, it is 3 o'clock and 12 o'clock is pointing straight up.

• Swing the pole from 2 o'clock to 12 o'clock and then back to 2 o'clock as you aim toward your target.

• The hook and bobber should land in the water where you were pointing.

When the bobber goes down, pull the cane pole up and set the hook! Hold on and pull that fish in!

TACKLE BOX
TUNE UP

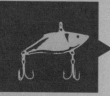

This is a great time to make sure your tackle box will be ready for next season.

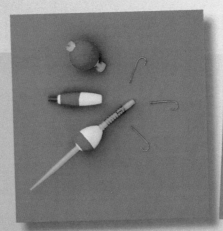

PANFISH/CRAPPIE

▷ Different types and sizes of bobbers

▷ Small, size 6 Aberdeen style hooks

▷ Different type and sizes of jigs-1/32 and 1/64 oz

▷ Split shot, in different sizes

▷ Fingernail clippers, to cut and trim line

▷ Tackle box to keep everything organized

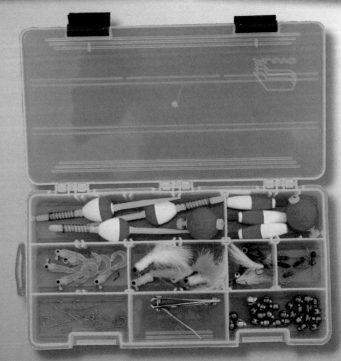

BASS

▶ 1/0 and 2/0 wide gap worm hooks

▶ Worm weights, in different sizes

▶ 4 to 7 inch worms in different colors

▶ Size 4 octopus style hooks

▶ 4 to 6 inch Senko style worms in different colors, to fish Wacky style

▶ Spinnerbaits

▶ Crankbaits

▶ Jigs

▶ Tackle box

SPINNERBAITS

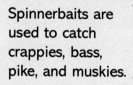

Spinnerbaits are used to catch crappies, bass, pike, and muskies.

Spinnerbaits use metal blades that spin like a propeller when the bait moves through the water. This creates shiny flashes and vibration that look and sound like small fish.

You can fish spinnerbaits in and around weeds, stumps, rocks, and docks. You can fish them shallow or in deep water.

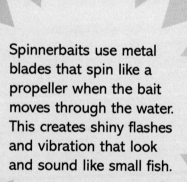

PARTS OF A SPINNERBAIT

Willow leaf blades come in different sizes and color. These blades are used to make the spinnerbait have more flash.

Colorado blades also come in different sizes, color, and finish. These blades make more vibration that fish can feel. You can fish these blades slower through the water.

The trailer hook is connected to main hook to help catch fish that may not get hooked with the main hook.

Attach line here

The weighted head can range from 1/8 ounce to 1 ounce.

The **skirt** goes on behind the weighted head. These come in all different colors and materials. They can be rubber, silicone, hair, and synthetic.

Trailers are used on trailer hook or the main hook. These add more action to the spinnerbait but are not always needed.

Pick your type of blade, skirt, and trailer. Tie it on, and go catch some big fish.

Gettin' Jiggy

> > > > > > > **JIG BASICS TO CATCH FISH**

Jig: a hook that has a weight in the front with rubber, soft plastic, hair, feathers, or other material attached to the hook.

Jigs >

< Jigs range in size from 1/32 oz. (really small), to 1 oz. (really big). The size of jig depends on the kind of fish you are fishing for. Crappie/Bluegill use small jigs. Bass use bigger jigs.

THERE ARE MANY WAYS TO FISH A JIG. TRY TO LEARN EACH WAY SO YOU CAN CATCH MORE FISH.

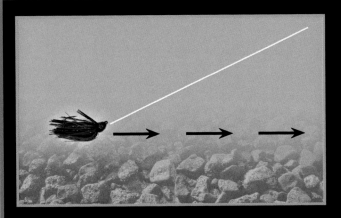

∧ Drag the jig on the bottom; stop it for 2-5 seconds, and then drag it again. Do this all the way back. This acts like a crawfish trying to escape.

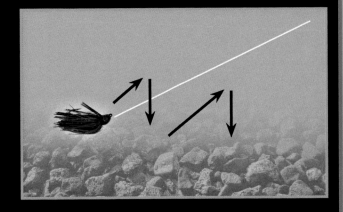

∧ Hop the jig off the bottom about 4-6 inches, then allow the jig to fall back to the bottom. Do this all the way back as you reel it in. This acts like an injured fish or other food that the fish may eat.

∧ Reel and swim the jig back to you, keeping the jig off the bottom. You can swim the jig over weeds, brush, or any other cover. This acts like a swimming fish trying to escape.

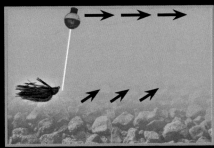

∧ Using a bobber, pull in the line with small jerks. Move the bobber only 2-3 inches at a time. This makes the jig go up and down, and acts like an injured fish.

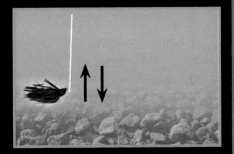

∧ Move the jig straight up, then let it fall back the bottom. This works good in thick cover and when fish are not very active.

PiCk a jig, PRaCtiCe these DiffeRent Ways, anD CatCh fish.

Knots to Know

Knots are used to connect your hooks and lures to your line. Practice tying these knots first using small rope. Then you will be ready to use these knots during your next fishing trip.

❶

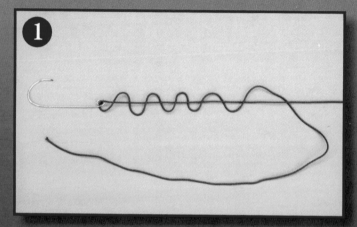

Improved Clinch knot

Easy to tie and very strong.

❶ Put the end of the line through the eye of the hook.

Make 5 turns or loops around the line.

❷ Take the end of the line through the first loop that is next to the eye.

❸ Then take the end of the line through the big loop.

❹ Wet the knot, and pull the end to tighten the knot. Slide the knot tightly next to the eye

❺ Clip extra line off.

❷

❸

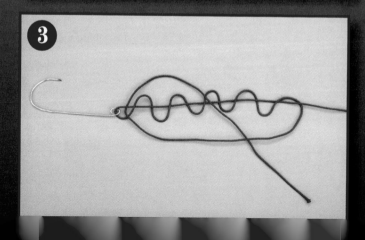

❹

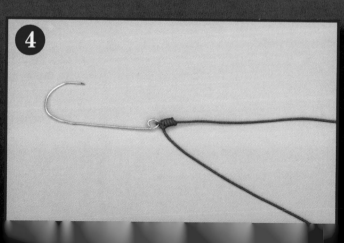

Palomar knot

Another popular knot, easy to tie and has 100% knot strength.

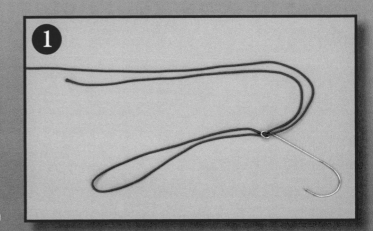

1. Double 4-6 inches of line and pass it through the eye of the hook

2. Tie an overhand knot with the double line, make sure the hook is hanging at the bottom.

3. Hold the overhand knot with finger and thumb.

4. Then pass the loop of line over the hook.

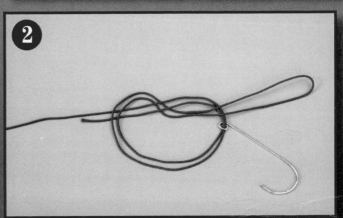

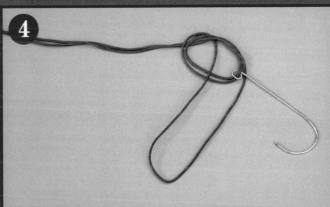

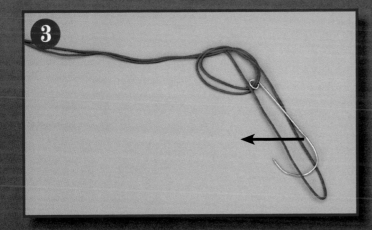

5. Pull both the line and tag end to tighten line down on to eye of hook.

6. Clip extra line off.

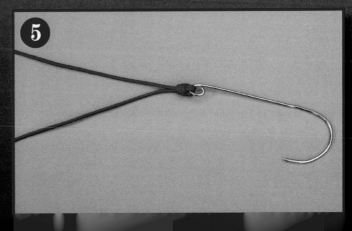

FLY FISHING GEAR

Fly Rod

These rods are very long and can be 7 to 9 feet in length. The long rod helps cast the line out. The size of the rod matches the size of line.

Fly Reel

This reel is used to store the line, but not used to cast out the line.

Fly Line

Fly line is heavier, thicker, and more bright colored than regular fishing line.

Fly line is measured in weights, they range from 1-12, with 6 being the most common.

Fly line can be floating, sinking, and floating with a sinking end. Floating line is the easiest to use.

Leader

A leader is a clear, thinner piece of line that attaches to the fly line.

The leader is then tied to the fly, and allows the fly to land softly on the water.

Waders

Waders are boots that keep you dry from your feet to your hips or chest.

This allows you to walk in streams without getting wet.

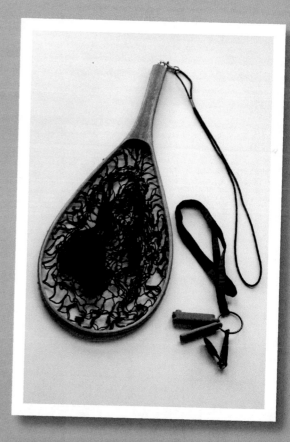

Nets

Fishing nets make it easier to land your fish when fishing, especially when wading in the water.

Clippers

Clippers help you cut your line when you need to change your fly.

Flies, Flies, EVERYWHERE!

What is a Fly?

A fly is a lure used to catch fish when you are fly-fishing. They are made using feathers, fur, hair, threads, and many other type of materials. Flies are made to look like bugs, fish, and anything that lives in or near the water.

Feathers, Fur, and Hair:

Feathers used to make flies can come from pheasant, goose, duck, turkey, and even an ostrich plume.

Fur and hair from squirrels, deer, bear, fox, rabbits, and even buffalo are used to make flies.

Threads and other Materials:

Many different colored threads, yarns, tinsel, rubber legs, and many other different type of materials help to keep the fly together and make it look alive.

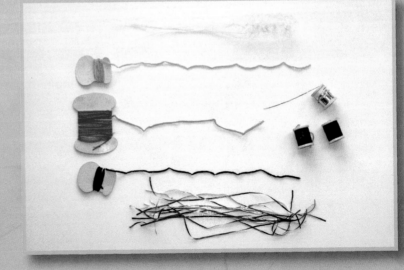

Major Types of Flies:

Dry Fly:

This fly is made to look like a natural insect floating on top of the water.

Nymph:

This fly looks like an insect in the larvae stage. A nymph is fished below the surface of the water.

Wet Fly:

This fly looks like a drowned or dying natural insect that is under the water.

Streamers and Bucktails:

These flies do not imitate an insect, they look more like a minnow or small fish. Streamers are made with feathers Bucktails are make with hair or fur.

How to Catch Fish Through the

ICE

THE BASICS OF ICE FISHING

Just because the lake or pond is covered with thick ice, doesn't mean you can't go fishing. Ice fishing is special type of fishing where you can catch fish that are swimming below several inches of ice. If you learn the basics, you can brave the cold and try your hand at catching fish through the ice.

SAFETY FIRST!!
- Never go onto a frozen lake or pond by yourself!! An adult MUST always go with you.
- Never walk onto a frozen lake or pond unless a grown up has tested the thickness of the ice. To safely walk on a frozen lake or pond, the ice must be MORE THAN 4 inches thick!

Once you know it is safe and you are with an adult, you will need some things to begin ice fishing.

- ice fishing poles and tackle (see pages 34-35)
- ice auger   • ice scoop   • bucket   • bait/ lures

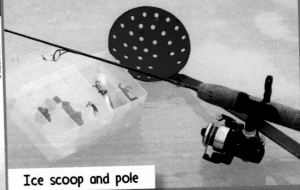

Ice scoop and pole

hand auger and ice scoop

drilling a hole by hand

Step 1:

Drill a hole in the ice where you want to fish. You drill the hole with an ice auger. Ice augers can be powered by hand or by an engine.

You should begin by drilling a hole near some type of cover like rocks or sunken trees because that is where fish like to hang out.

You can really go high tech and use an electronic fish-finder to locate the fish under the ice. When you find the fish, you drill the hole.

Step 2:

Set up your rod and choose your bait or lure. The bait or lure will depend on the type of fish you are trying to catch.

Panfish like small worms or larva like waxworms and grubs. Larger fish like bass, walleye and pike like minnows. You can also use artificial lures like jigs to catch fish through the ice.

Here a fun thing to try: Find your own bait by looking for goldenrod grubs. These small grubs can be found inside the swollen stems of goldenrod.

artificial worms and dry salted minnows

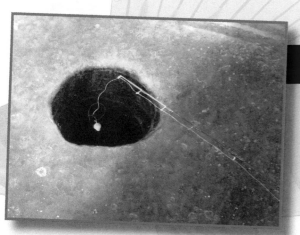

goldenrod galls in field

tiny worm in gall

Step 3:

Watch your bobber or line and wait for a bite. You can also slowly move the bait up and down and feel for the fish biting the bait or lure.

Be alert!! When fish are cold, they usually nibble lightly and do not move much when they take the bait.

Staying Warm

Be sure you dress warmly when you go out ice fishing. It can get pretty cold on the ice in the winter time.

If you are real serious, you can get portable shelters that you can take out onto the ice. These tiny tents or houses are called ice shanties. You can even put a heater in them to stay warm!!

Success!!

If you are patient and the fish are biting, you may go home with a mess of fish to eat. Ice fishing is a great cure for cabin fever after you may have been inside for a while during the cold winter months.

Remember go with a grown up, stay safe and have fun trying this fun way of fishing!

ice fishing gear

▶ **Rod and Reels:**

• Ice rods are usually very short, less than 24 inches in length.

• Can use your light action spinning reel.

• Jig poles and reels are very simple and work well.

Common ice fishing rod and reel

Another type of ice fishing rod and reel

©istock/Dick Stada

▶ **Fishing Line:**

• 2 – 6 pound test for panfish, crappie, and perch.

• 6-12 pound test for bass, walleye, and pike.

Tip-ups:

- A tip-up is a device that sits in the ice hole with your line and bait.

- When a fish bites, a flag "tips up" to let you know you have a bite.

- This allows you to leave that fishing hole and fish in another one.

Tip up rig

©istock/Brian Faust

Jigs, hooks, spoons, and lures

Hooks:
- #10-12 small hooks for panfish

- #3 short shank hook for walleyes.

- 2/0 hooks and up for Northern Pike.

Jigs:
- Can use minnow imitating jigs.

Different types of ice jigs and lures.

Small lures:
- Small ice flies, teardrops, and other small jigs that are used with live bait.

Spoons:
- Used with live bait for bigger fish.

Split shot:
- To help get your hook and bait to the fish.

Don't forget about using a bobber or a spring bobber to help you know when you have a bite.

Outdoor Youth Opportunties and Programs

There are many organizations that offer wonderful programs and opportunities for young people to experience and learn more about fishing skills and the outdoors in fun and hands on ways. Here are a few that are offered across the nation that you may be able to find and attend close to where you live.

Take Me Fishing Initiative

 Take Me Fishing is an iniative of the Recreational Boating and Fishing Foundation's (RBFF). Take Me Fishing announces three great new patches for Cub Scouts and Boy Scouts to earn while sharing their love of angling. It's fun, it's easy and it's right at your fingertips.

Passport Patch

 The Passport Patch program is an introduction to fishing and boating for Cub Scouts. Scouts take part in a fun and exciting six step interactive program that teaches various skills every angler needs to be knowledgeable, safe, and confident while fishing and boating.

First Catch Patch

 Cub Scouts and Boy Scouts can earn this patch by organizing a real-life fishing trip. The First Catch program is a great follow-up to the Passport Patch program, or can be done as a stand-alone program.

Mentor Patch

 This distinctive patch is for Boy Scouts who organize a fishing trip for newcomers to the sport. The Mentor Patch program develops leadership qualities and introduces someone new to the wonderful world of fishing and boating.

To inspire a love of boating and fishing at an early age, the Take Me Fishing™ campaign also teamed up with Discovery Education and The Sports Authority to introduce Explore the Blue. This interactive program and website (ExploretheBlue.com) brings on-the-water experiences to life through cross-curricular lesson plans, printable outdoor activities for the family, and an interactive boating and fishing game called 'Thrill of the Catch.'

For more info on the programs offered by Take Me Fishing, visit http://www.takemefishing.org/community/scouting/home

Trailblazer Adventure Program

 The Trailblazer Adventure program is offered at locations across the nation by the United States Sportsman's Alliance Foundation (USSAF). The program is the largest youth outdoor sports introduction program in America. This one-day program serves as an all-around introduction to the thrill of outdoor sports and the importance of conservation. It is typically hosted at a Boy Scout camp or similar facility. The Trailblazer Adventure Day features a variety of activities, demonstrations and orientation sessions designed to show children and their parents what the outdoor lifestyle is all about. Activities include firearm safety, archery, trapping, fishing and much more. All activities are conducted under the supervision of experienced Trail Guides with an emphasis on safety. Find out more at http://ussportsmen.org/page.aspx?pid=261

The Bass Federation

The Bass Federation (TBF) is the oldest and largest organized grass roots fishing organization in the country with three main principles, Fishing, Youth, and Conservation. One of the oldest and most productive programs that the Bass Federation has ever had is the TBF Junior Angler Program. In this program young anglers from 11-18 are members of an active junior fishing clubs that are sponsored by TBF adult Bass Clubs. We have active state Junior Programs in 40 states across the country.

The Bass Federation and its member states have implemented a casting skills accuracy challenge for young anglers across the country! "The Reel Kids Program" is in many cases the first opportunity that many kids have to be introduced to the great sport of fishing. At events like sport and outdoor shows across the country and in many schools these programs are giving kids the chance to experience what it is really like to handle a fishing rod and reel. They test their skills in the art of Casting, Flipping, and Pitching a plastic jig to a very colorful target.

To find out more about these programs, visit http://bassfederation.com/tbf-youth/.

B.A.S.S. Junior Bassmasters Program

The Bass Anglers Sportsman Society or BASS was founded by Ray Scott with simple goals in mind; to create an honest fishing tournament trail, improve our environment by bringing together anglers, and to keep a bright fishing future for our youth. Today, BASS Federation Nation hosts the largest tournament fishing event in the nation, the Bassmasters.

One of the most exciting opportunities BASS has created for young anglers is the Junior Bassmaster World Championship (JWC). Just like mom or dad competing in the BASS Federation Nation okc competitions, this program allows junior members the opportunity to compete at a club, state and divisional level, and eventually qualifying them for their own Junior Bassmaster World Championship. The competition looks like the BASS Federation Nation tournaments. The youth anglers gain a variety to the skills as they participate.

Youth competitors also have a chance to qualify as members of their adult state team. Juniors are mentored by Federation Nation anglers and learn the skills and principle that are important to the BASS Federation Nation.

In 1991, BASS developed the Bassmaster CastingKids program, which is similar to the NFL punt, pass and kick events. However, in CastingKids the challenge is to flip, pitch and cast with accuracy. Mastering these three techniques will give any angler the skills they need to present lures and catch bass.

CastingKids is now going to introduce even more youth through a partnership with the U.S. Sportsmen's Alliance Foundation's Adventure Trailblazer events. With CastingKids changing from a competition-based focus to an education-focused program, it's now going to teach the basics of fishing to much larger groups through the Trailblazer events already being held at Scout Camps and other facilities across the county.

To find out more about BASS and the Junior Bassmasters Program visit http://www.bassmaster.com/news/all-about-junior-bassmaster.

Trout Unlimited

Trout Unlimited's Stream Explorer membership offers kids a chance to learn about wild fish and the natural world. Now more than ever, kids need to be encouraged to get outside and discover the fascinating life of trout and salmon and the rivers where

they live. A Stream Explorers membership is a positive step toward creating the next generation of environmental caretakers. Benefits include issues of Stream Explorers or Trout magazine, stickers, a Trout Unlimited wall calendar, and a Trout Unlimited membership card. Check out the Stream Explorers website at https://www.tumembership.org/youth.

Trout Unlimited (TU) also provides Trout in the Classroom that offers students of all ages a chance to raise trout in a classroom setting and then release them into a nearby stream or river. During the eight months that classes spend raising trout, they closely monitor water temperature, water clarity, dissolved oxygen, ammonia levels, and pH. Because trout are extremely sensitive to changes in their environment, students learn the importance of clean water and protecting the environment. TU also offers 17 Youth Conservation Camps and Academies across the country, all of which are organized and ran by committed Trout Unlimited volunteers. These streamside, hands-on experiences provide more than just casting and fishing lessons, they educate youth about the complex issues behind restoring and protecting our streams and rivers. Visit TU's website for more information at http://www.tu.org/about-us/youth.

INDEX